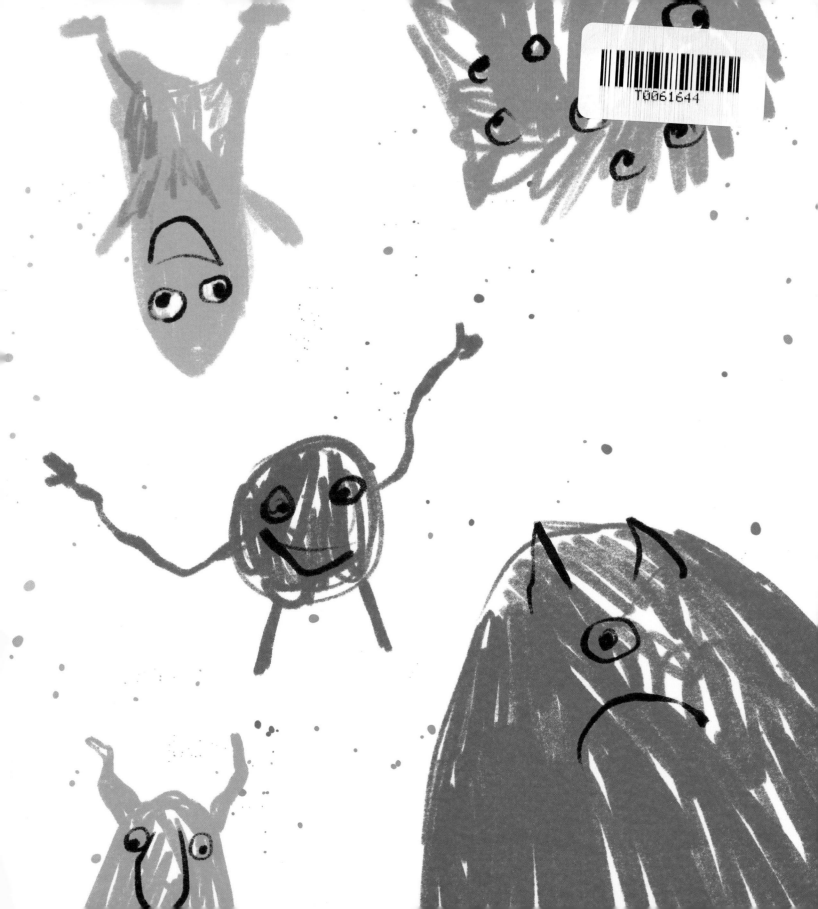

I am so grateful to my husband, Dennis, and my children, Lauren and Ryan, for all their support! I appreciate the encouragement of so many friends and the inspiration and advice from my friend and colleague Chris Willard. Finally, a shout-out to Mayo School in Holden, Massachusetts, where my early teachings were so warmly welcomed!

Bala Kids
An imprint of Shambhala Publications, Inc.
2129 13th Street
Boulder, Colorado 80302
www.shambhala.com

9 8 7 6 5 4 3 2 1

First Edition
Printed in China

♾ This edition is printed on acid-free paper that meets the American National Standards Institute Z39.48 Standard.
♻ Shambhala Publications makes every effort to print on postconsumer recycled paper. For more information please visit www.shambhala.com.
Bala Kids is distributed worldwide by Penguin Random House, Inc., and its subsidiaries.

Library of Congress Cataloging-in-Publication Data
Names: O'Leary, Wendy, author. | Landry, Noémie Gionet, illustrator.
Title: The monster parade: a book about feeling all your feelings and then watching them go / Wendy O'Leary ; illustrated by Noémie Gionet Landry.
Description: Boulder, Colorado: Bala Kids, [2022]
Identifiers: LCCN 2020042604 | ISBN 9781611809220 (board)
Subjects: LCSH: Emotions in children—Juvenile literature. | Emotions—Juvenile literature.
Classification: LCC BF723.E6 O44 2022 | DDC 155.4/124—dc23
LC record available at https://lccn.loc.gov/2020042604

THE MONSTER PARADE

A Book about Feeling All Your
Feelings and Then Watching Them Go

Wendy O'Leary
Illustrated by Noémie Gionet Landry

bala kids

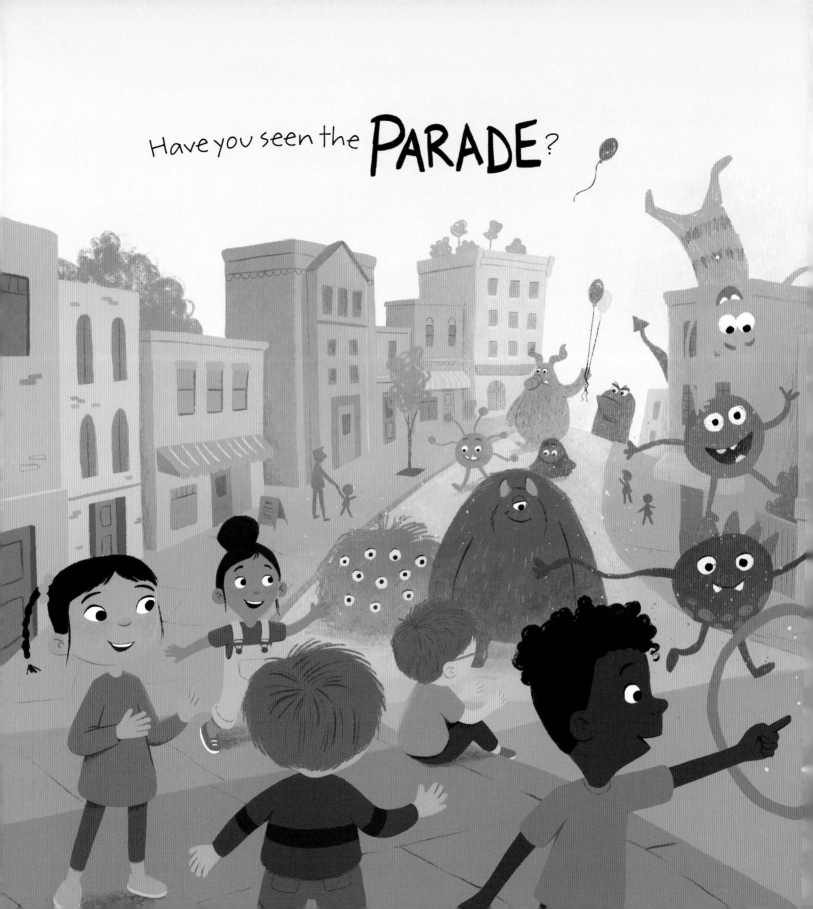

Have you seen the PARADE?

It happens all day.
Wherever you are,
   it will come your way.

Sometimes it is

SCARY...

...and then it's such

FUN!

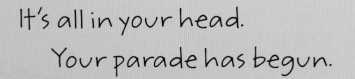

It's all in your head.
Your parade has begun.

Here's the **ANGRY** monster, headed this way.

It growls so loud,
but you know it won't stay.

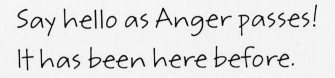

Say hello as Anger passes!
It has been here before.

Don't jump in and join it.
Feel your feet on the floor.

If your body feels tight,
and you just want to

SCREAM,

walk as you breathe.
Put the parade on a screen.

Now there's big
SADNESS,
heavy, slow, and so gray.

A lump in your throat,
but you won't float away.

You don't join the parade.

Your **BREATH** keeps you here.

Follow it in and then out.
Watch Sadness disappear.

Breathe in and your belly
fills like a balloon.
Breathe out and it shrinks.

You will feel CALMER so soon.

As the feelings march by,
some may seem really scary.

LARGE,

DARK,

and

LOUD—

could they even be hairy?

Sneaking around
the corner are

WORRY and

FEAR.

Notice your body now.

They may soon disappear.

Just remember
a time you felt
HAPPY
and
BRIGHT.

After you notice hard feelings,
it will help you feel light.

Notice a **WONDERFUL** thing that happens each day.

It can move the parade quickly.
Sad feelings drift away.

Sit **STILL** and so **QUIET.**

Count your breath to three.

Notice how you feel now
and then let it be.

Feelings are just feelings . . .
they come and then go.

But the GOODNESS inside
will continue to show.

Watch your parade
of emotions,
        the old and the new.

As it passes on by,
just take in the view!

Practices

Like everyone, you probably have really big feelings sometimes, and *The Monster Parade* is a reminder of a few things that can help.

Can you think of a time when you felt sad or angry or scared? Did you notice that those feelings also went away? That's right—feelings come and go . . . and you can handle them, just like you have before.

Everyone has feelings. Remember you can notice who is in the parade without joining it or stopping it. You can give each feeling a name and imagine what it looks like, and maybe even notice how it feels in your body. This is just a feeling that is happening right now, and you can let it pass.

Once you notice a difficult feeling, you can also try to pay attention to something that makes you feel good. Taking charge of where you put your attention and focusing on things that make you happy can make a big difference.

It is great to be curious about your emotions. You can be like a detective trying to notice, name, and be curious about these interesting monsters in your parade.

And always remember: you are more than your feelings.

HERE ARE A FEW EXERCISES TO TRY:

Name It to Tame It

Naming a feeling helps the alarm system in our brain calm down. There are lots of ways to practice naming and getting to know your feelings.

- Draw a picture of one feeling or the parade of feelings.
- Give each feeling a name.
- Make clay creatures or stick puppets that represent each feeling.
- Ask questions:

  What does it feel like when Anger is going by in the parade?

  What does my body look like when Fear is passing?

  How can I tell which emotions are in someone else's parade?

Feel It in Your Body

When you are noticing a strong emotion, see if you can tell where it is in your body. What does it feel like? Does it stay the same or change when you shine some attention on it?

Feet on the Floor

Notice your feet on the floor and see if that makes you feel calm and strong. Imagine you are a tree and your feet are roots that go deep into the ground, or that you are a mountain rising out of the earth.

Use the Parade Idea

- Which feelings are in your parade?
- Can you watch as the parade goes by?
- Can you put the parade on a computer or television screen?
- Can you draw a picture of it and name the different characters?
- Make a parade with your class or family. Put on music and have everyone march as an angry or happy or silly monster. (Parade monsters always keep their hands to themselves.)

Breathing Practices

Try some breathing exercises for calming.

Belly Breath

Imagine there is a balloon in your belly. When you breathe in your belly gets bigger as if you are filling it up, and when you breathe out it gets smaller as if you are letting the air out.

Counting Breath

Adding words while paying attention to breathing can be helpful. Count each breath and go up to five (*in one, out one, in two, out two . . .*). You can also use a word that may be helpful (*in calm, out peaceful . . .*).

Author's Note

The parade works for grown-ups too! Before writing this story, I used the idea of a parade when I taught both children and adults about noticing and working with emotions and sticky thoughts. Big feelings are a part of life for all of us. Seeing emotions as simply moving in a parade is a great way to remember that they are only passing—we don't need to get stuck or even follow them. It also helps us see our emotions in a playful way and with some kindness and interest. I have found it really helpful to use the parade analogy in my own life! For example, when I notice I am feeling worried, I remember the parade and see a googly-eyed Worry creature. Then I say to myself, "Yes, I see you. And you can continue along the parade now." Often I can even give the characters in my parade a little smile as they pass; they come and go, *and* we can handle them.

The tools in this story should help you notice and welcome your emotions and then let them pass.

Wendy O'Leary, MEd, is an educator, public speaker, and author who teaches skills to support emotional intelligence, regulation, and resiliency. Wendy has taught in hundreds of classrooms, has presented at conferences and professional development trainings, and has been a guest lecturer for undergraduate classes. In addition to her work with children, Wendy also facilitates groups and classes for youths and adults in mindfulness and related topics. Her first children's book, *Breathing Makes It Better*, co-authored with Christopher Willard, was published in the fall of 2019.

Noémie Gionet Landry grew up in a small coastal town of New-Brunswick, Canada, surrounded by the ocean. Growing up, she told everyone she wanted to become either a doctor or a children's book illustrator. Midway through med school, she decided she would do both. She now shares her time between the hospital (where she works as a rheumatologist) and her home studio, where she sketches, draws, and paints, surrounded by her wife, two tiny Chihuahua, and two cats.